A GREAT LEADER TO INFLUENCE OTHERS

Proven Way To Lead People Uprightly Without Stress

Book Description

Book Overview

In this "**A Great Leader To Influence Others**

"

The experience in this book is to influence anyone positively and create a positive and strong relationship for others to imitate.

It keeps increasing your ability to get things done by building trust and rapport.

This book teaches about skills for success in both personal and professional relationships. This book teaches how a great leader to first understand people perspective and values to things

INTRODUCTION

A great leader influence others while persuading people to the point of view, handling conflicts and criticism, and becoming a leader and a friend are essential skills for success in both personal and professional relationships. Whether you are trying to convince someone to see things from your perspective, navigating a disagreement, or inspiring others to follow your lead, these skills are crucial for effective communication and relationship-building.

 it is important as a great leader to first understood the listener perspective and values. By empathizing with their position, you can tailor your arguments to resonate with their beliefs and priorities. It is also important to present your ideas with confidence and clarity, using evidence and reasoning to support your stance. Additionally, active listening and open-

mindedness can help you build rapport and trust with others, making them more receptive to your ideas.

When handling conflicts and criticism, it is important to remain calm and composed. Rather than reacting defensively, try to understand the other person's concerns and find common ground for resolution.

Constructive feedback should be seen as an opportunity for growth, and it is important to approach it with humility and a willingness to learn and improve.

Becoming a leader and a friend involves building strong relationships based on trust, respect, and effective communication. A good leader inspires and motivates others, while also being open to feedback and collaboration. A good friend is supportive, empathetic, and trustworthy, and values the well-being and happiness of others.

In conclusion, mastering the art of persuasion, conflict resolution, and leadership is essential for building strong and meaningful relationships. By approaching these skills with empathy, open-mindedness, and a willingness to learn and grow,

you can become a more effective communicator and a trusted friend and leader.

CHAPTER 1

HANDLING CONFLICTS AND CRITICISM, AND BECOMING A LEADER.

Handling conflicts and criticism is an essential skill for personal and professional growth. When we face any conflicts, it is important to approach the situation with an open mind and a willingness to understand the perspectives of all parties involved. Active listening and effective communication are key in resolving conflicts, as they allow for a deeper understanding of the underlying issues and help in finding common ground for resolution.

When dealing with criticism, it's important to remain open to feedback and view it as an opportunity for self-improvement. Rather than becoming defensive, take the time to reflect on the feedback and consider how it can help you grow and develop. Constructive criticism can provide valuable insights that can lead to personal and professional advancement.

Becoming a leader involves not only guiding and inspiring others but also being a good listener and collaborator. Effective leaders are able to Communicate their vision, motivate their team, and lead by example. They also foster a positive and inclusive environment where everyone feels valued and empowered to contribute their ideas and skills.

In summary, handling conflicts and criticism with an open mind and a willingness to learn and grow, and becoming a leader who inspires and supports others, are crucial skills for personal and professional success. By mastering these skills, you can build strong relationships, foster a positive work environment, and achieve your goals as a leader.

Impactful environment is crucial in your personal and professional life

CHAPTER 2

TRYING TO CONVINCE SOMEONE TO SEE THINGS FROM YOUR PERSPECTIVE, NAVIGATING A DISAGREEMENT

When trying to convince someone to see things from your perspective or navigating a disagreement, it's important to approach the situation with empathy,

patience, and effective communication. Here are some tips to help you navigate these challenging conversations:

1. ***Understand their perspective***: Take your time to listen actively and understand the other person's point of view. Show empathy and acknowledge their feelings and concerns. Understanding their perspective will help you tailor your arguments and find common ground.

2. ***Communicate clearly and respectfully***: Clearly articulate your perspective and the reasons behind your beliefs or decisions. Use respectful language and avoid being confrontational. Focus on the facts and try to avoid emotional responses.

3. ***Find common ground***: Look for areas of agreement or shared goals. Emphasize the points where your perspectives align and use them as a foundation for finding a resolution.

4. ***Be open to compromise***: In some cases, finding a middle ground may be the best solution. Be willing to make concessions and seek a solution that benefits both parties.

5. ***Stay calm and patient***: Emotions can run high during disagreements, but it's important

to remain calm and patient. Take a step back if needed and avoid escalating the situation.

6. ***Seek understanding, not just agreement***: Sometimes, the goal may not be to change the other person's mind, but to ensure that they understand your perspective. Mutual understanding can lead to mutual respect, even if you don't fully agree.

7. ***Focus on the issue, not the person***: When discussing differing perspectives, it's crucial to focus on the specific issue at hand and avoid personal attacks or criticism.

By approaching these conversations with empathy, respect, and a willingness to find common ground, you can increase the likelihood of successfully convincing someone to see things from your perspective or navigating a disagreement in a constructive manner.

CHAPTER3

TO PERSUADE PEOPLE TO YOUR POINT OF VIEW

To effectively persuade people to your point of view, it's important to employ a combination of communication skills, empathy, and well-reasoned

arguments. Here are some strategies to help you persuade others:

1. ***Understand their perspective***: Before attempting to persuade someone, take the time to understand their perspective. What are their values, concerns, and priorities? By understanding where they're coming from, you can tailor your arguments to resonate with their beliefs.

2. ***Build rapport***: Establishing a positive and respectful relationship with the person you're trying to persuade can make them more receptive to your viewpoint. Show empathy, listen actively, and demonstrate that you value their input.

3. ***Use evidence and reasoning***: When presenting your arguments, support them with evidence, facts, and logical reasoning. This can help make your case more compelling and credible.

4. ***Appeal to emotions***: While evidence and logic are important, emotions also play a significant role in persuasion. Appeal to the emotions and values of the person you're trying to persuade to make your argument more relatable and impactful.

5. ***Be confident and clear***: Present your ideas with confidence and clarity. Uncertainty can undermine your persuasive efforts, so it's important to communicate your position with conviction.

6. ***Address counterarguments***: Anticipate potential counterarguments and address them proactively. Demonstrating that you've considered alternative viewpoints can strengthen your position and show that you've thought critically about the issue.

7. ***Be patient and respectful***: Persuasion often takes time, and it's important to be patient and respectful throughout the process. Avoid being aggressive or confrontational, as this can create resistance rather than receptivity.

By combining these strategies, you can enhance your ability to persuade others to see things from your perspective. Remember that effective persuasion is not about forcing your views on others but about engaging in respectful and constructive dialogue.

CHAPTER 4

PRESENT YOUR IDEAS WITH CONFIDENCE AND CLARITY, USING EVIDENCE AND REASONING TO SUPPORT YOUR VIEW POINT

Absolutely, presenting ideas with confidence and clarity, backed by evidence and reasoning, is crucial for effective communication and persuasion. Here's an example of how this might be applied in a professional context:

Suppose you are advocating for the implementation of a new project management system within your organization. Here's how you could present your viewpoint with confidence and clarity, using evidence and reasoning to support your argument:

"I believe that implementing a new project management system will significantly improve our team's efficiency and productivity. The current system has led to several instances of miscommunication and missed deadlines. To support this, a recent study by [reputable source] found that companies that adopted similar systems experienced a 20% increase in project completion rates.

Furthermore, the user feedback we collected highlighted specific pain points with the current

system, such as the lack of real-time collaboration features and difficulty in tracking project milestones. These issues have directly impacted our ability to deliver projects on time and within budget.

By transitioning to a new project management system, we can address these challenges and streamline our project workflows. The system we are proposing offers advanced collaboration tools, automated task tracking, and real-time progress monitoring, as evidenced by positive case studies from similar organizations in our industry.

I understand that change can be daunting, but the potential benefits of this new system, as supported by the evidence and experiences of other companies, far outweigh the initial adjustment period. I am confident that this investment will lead to improved project outcomes and ultimately contribute to our long-term success."

In this example, the speaker uses a confident and clear tone, supports their viewpoint with evidence from reputable sources and user feedback, and employs reasoning to demonstrate the potential benefits of the proposed change. This approach can help build a compelling case and increase the likelihood of persuading others to adopt the new project management system.

CHAPTER 5

BECOMING A LEADER AND A FRIEND INVOLVES BUILDING STRONG RELATIONSHIPS

Absolutely, building strong relationships is fundamental to becoming a leader and a friend. Here are some key principles to consider when aiming building strong relationships:

1. ***Trust and Integrity***: Trust is the foundation of any strong relationship. As a leader and a friend, it's essential to demonstrate integrity, honesty, and reliability to earn and maintain the trust of others.

2. ***Empathy and Understanding***: Both in leadership and friendship, empathy and understanding are vital. Being able to see things from others' perspectives, actively listening, and showing genuine care and concern fosters strong connections.

3. ***Communication***: Open, honest, and effective communication is key. As a leader, clear communication helps to convey expectations, provide feedback, and inspire others. In

friendships, communication builds understanding and connection.

4. ***Support and Encouragement***: Offering support and encouragement is essential in both leadership and friendships. Being there for others in times of need and celebrating their successes strengthens relationships.

5. ***Collaboration and Teamwork***: In leadership, promoting collaboration and teamwork fosters a sense of unity and shared purpose. In friendships, working together and sharing experiences can deepen bonds.

6. ***Respect and Appreciation***: Showing respect for others' opinions, boundaries, and contributions is crucial. Additionally, expressing appreciation for the people in your life strengthens relationships and fosters a positive environment.

7. ***Consistency and Reliability***: Being consistent and reliable in your actions and words builds trust and confidence in both leadership and friendships.

By embodying these principles, you can develop and nurture strong relationships, whether in a leadership role or in your personal life. Strong

relationships are the cornerstone of effective leadership and meaningful friendships.

CHAPTER 6

MASTERING THE ART OF PERSUASION, CONFLICT RESOLUTION, AND LEADERSHIP

Mastering the art of persuasion, conflict resolution, and leadership involves a combination of skills, strategies, and mindset. Here's a breakdown of key elements for each of these areas:

1. Persuasion:

    - ***Effective Communication***: Mastering the art of persuasion begins with strong communication skills. This includes active listening, clear articulation of ideas, and the ability to tailor messages to resonate with different audiences.
    - ***Building Credibility***: Establishing credibility through expertise, trustworthiness, and integrity is essential for successful persuasion. Backing up arguments with evidence

- o and reasoning also strengthens your position.
- o ***Understanding Emotions and Values***: Persuasion often involves appealing to emotions and values. Understanding what motivates and influences others can enhance your ability to persuade effectively.

Empathy and Respect: Demonstrating empathy and respect for others' viewpoints, even when they differ from your own, can foster a more receptive environment for persuasion.

2. ***Conflict Resolution***:

- o ***Active Listening***: Effective conflict resolution starts with active listening to understand the perspectives and concerns of all parties involved.
- o ***Collaboration and Compromise***: Encouraging collaboration and seeking mutually beneficial solutions can help resolve conflicts constructively.
- o ***Emotional Intelligence***: Being aware of emotions, managing them effectively, and understanding the emotions of others are crucial aspects of successful conflict resolution.

- *Mediation and Negotiation*: Developing skills in mediation and negotiation can be valuable for resolving conflicts in various settings.

Leadership:

Vision and Inspiration: Effective leaders articulate a compelling vision and inspire others to work towards common goals.

- *Emotional Intelligence*: Understanding and managing one's own emotions, as well as being attuned to the emotions of others, is a key aspect of successful leadership.
- *Decision-Making and Problem-Solving*: Strong leaders are adept at making sound decisions and solving complex problems, often by leveraging input from diverse perspectives.
- *Empowerment and Support*: Empowering others, providing support, and fostering a positive, inclusive environment are hallmarks of effective leadership.

Mastering these areas requires ongoing learning, practice, and self-reflection. By honing these skills

and adopting a growth mindset, individuals can become more effective persuaders, adept conflict resolvers, and impactful leaders.

CONCLUSION

In conclusion, becoming a great leader who can influence others is a multifaceted journey that involves a combination of key attributes, skills, and a commitment to continuous growth. A great leader inspires and motivates others, fosters a positive and inclusive environment, and drives meaningful change. Here are some key points to consider:

1. ***Vision and Purpose***: A great leader communicates a compelling vision and purpose, inspiring others to rally around common goals and aspirations.

2. ***Empathy and Emotional Intelligence***: Understanding the emotions and perspectives of others, and demonstrating empathy, is crucial for building strong connections and trust.

3. ***Communication and Persuasion***: Effective communication skills, coupled with the ability to persuade and influence, are

essential for conveying ideas, aligning teams, and driving change.

4. ***Integrity and Trustworthiness***: Upholding integrity, being transparent, and maintaining

trust are foundational elements of great leadership.

5. ***Adaptability and Resilience***: Great leaders are adaptable in the face of change, resilient in times of

adversity, and capable of guiding others through challenges.

6. Empowerment and Support: Empowering others, providing support, and fostering a culture of collaboration and growth are central to a great leader's influence.

7. Continuous Learning and Development: A commitment to ongoing learning, self-improvement, and seeking feedback is vital for personal and professional growth as a leader.

Influence is earned through actions, consistency, and the positive impact a leader has on those around them. By embodying these attributes and continually developing these skills, individuals can become great leaders who inspire and influence others to achieve collective success.